FOR **LIFE**.
SMALL GROUPS

WELCOME
HOME CONNECTING AND ENGAGING
PEOPLE IN THE CHURCH

MICHAEL KELLEY
& THOM S. RAINER

LifeWay Press® • Nashville, Tennessee

© 2018 LifeWay Press®

ISBN: 978-1-5359-1803-9
Item: 005806155

Dewey Decimal Classification: 254.5
Subject Headings: CHURCH \ EVANGELISTIC WORK \ DISCIPLESHIP

Eric Geiger
Senior Vice President, LifeWay Christian Resources

Gena Rogers
Brian Gass
Content Editors

Michael Kelley
Director, Groups Ministry

Send questions/comments to: Content Editor, *Bible Studies for Life: Adults*, One LifeWay Plaza, Nashville, TN 37234; or make comments on the Web at BibleStudiesforLife.com.

Printed in the United States of America.

For ordering or inquiries, visit lifeway.com; write LifeWay Small Groups; One LifeWay Plaza; Nashville, TN 37234; or call toll free (800) 458-2772.

We believe that the Bible has God for its author; salvation for its end; and truth, without any mixture of error, for its matter and that all Scripture is totally true and trustworthy. To review LifeWay's doctrinal guideline, please visit lifeway.com/doctrinalguideline.

All Scripture quotations, unless otherwise indicated, are taken from the the Christian Standard Bible®. Copyright 2018 by Holman Bible Publishers. Used by permission.

Bible Studies for Life: Adults often lists websites that may be helpful to our readers. Our staff verifies each site's usefulness and appropriateness prior to publication. However, website content changes quickly so we encourage you to approach all websites with caution. Make sure sites are still appropriate before sharing them with students, friends, and family.

contents

Social Media

 Connect with a community of *Bible Studies for Life* users. Post responses to questions, share teaching ideas, and link to great blog content. **facebook.com/biblestudiesforlife**

 Get instant updates about new articles, giveaways, and more. **@BibleMeetsLife**

The App

Bible Studies for Life is also available as an eBook. The eBook can be opened and read with the *Bible Studies for Life App*, a free app from the iOS App Store or the Google Play Store.

Blog

At **biblestudiesforlife.com/blog** you will find additional resources for your study experience, including music downloads provided by LifeWay Worship. Plus, leaders and group members alike will benefit from the blog posts written for people in every life stage—singles, parents, boomers, and senior adults—as well as media clips, connections between our study topics, current events, and much more.

Training

 For helps on how to use Bible Studies for Life, tips on how to better lead groups, or additional ideas for leading this session, visit: **ministrygrid.com/web/biblestudiesforlife.**

There's no place like home.

The most powerful communication tools we have at our disposal are often not our words. Experts in communication consistently tell us that much of our communication is presented in a non-verbal way.

▶ The teenager who says, "Yes, Sir," yet rolls her eyes.

▶ The teacher who says he values interaction but lectures in a monotone voice without ever pausing for questions.

▶ The job candidate who claims confidence in her ability to do the job but fidgets in her seat with the only break being nervous laughter.

These people are all saying *something*, but what they are *communicating* is quite different from what they are saying.

What are we communicating to those who come to our church or Bible study group for the very first time? What are we *really* saying? We might be verbalizing words of welcome, but we might also be presenting a message that says just the opposite.

In this study, we will examine what we are *really* saying. We will look deeply into the posture and attitude that exemplifies the right kind of invitation. We will look at what we need to do so that, when we encounter those who are just beginning to come around to the truth of God and His church, they don't just hear, but also *feel* the same welcome God has given us in Christ.

"You are welcome. We're glad you are here."

Michael Kelley

Michael serves as the Director of Groups Ministry at LifeWay Christian Resources, and is the author of *Boring, Wednesdays Were Pretty Normal*, and recently released a new book, *Growing Down*.

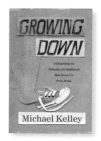

Thom Rainer

Thom serves as president and CEO of LifeWay Christian Resources. He publishes a daily blog and twice weekly podcast at ThomRainer. com. This study complements his new book, *Becoming a Welcoming Church*.

1 REALITY CHECK

What makes a house feel like a home?

QUESTION #1

Our lives should serve as a welcome mat into the church.

THE BIBLE MEETS LIFE

If you're like me, you could practically get home with your eyes closed. You've made the trip so many times you know it by heart: the bumps in the road, the places to turn, and even the way the sun shines through the trees.

So imagine one day you take this same road. You come to your house but when you get inside everything is different. The pictures on the wall have been replaced. The furniture is arranged the wrong way. Even the smell is different. The address is right, the house is correct, yet everything is off.

Many people feel the same way when they enter the church building. They've heard Jesus is a friend of sinners and God loves the world. They've been led to believe the people in church are friendly, and yet when they enter the building, they find something entirely inconsistent with those things they've heard.

We might think we're welcoming, but the reality can be entirely different. To ensure we're a welcoming church, let's go back to the beginning. We welcome others because of the gospel.

WHAT DOES THE BIBLE SAY?

Titus 3:3-8a

³ For we too were once foolish, disobedient, deceived, enslaved by various passions and pleasures, living in malice and envy, hateful, detesting one another. ⁴ But when the kindness of God our Savior and his love for mankind appeared, ⁵ he saved us—not by works of righteousness that we had done, but according to his mercy—through the washing of regeneration and renewal by the Holy Spirit. ⁶ He poured out his Spirit on us abundantly through Jesus Christ our Savior ⁷ so that, having been justified by his grace, we may become heirs with the hope of eternal life. ⁸ᵃ This saying is trustworthy.

Titus was on his own. He had traveled with Paul, seen the power of the gospel to change people's lives, and even carried a letter from Paul to the church at Corinth. He had been a trusted companion of the greatest missionary the world has ever known, but now he was by himself.

Paul had left Titus on the island of Crete to organize and carry out the beginning of the church there. Surely with an assignment like that—in a place that was foreign to both the gospel and Judaism—Titus would have had many questions about his role: What does it mean to be a pastor? How do I set up the work of ministry? What should I do *first*?

Paul addressed practical questions like these in his letter to Titus, but along with answers to practical ministry questions, Paul also reminded Titus of something that was already very familiar to him: the gospel. So, with all the pressing questions of how to do the work of the church in Crete, why would Paul pause to remind Titus of something he already knew? We see three reasons in this passage:

> *How have you personally experienced the kindness and love of God?*

QUESTION #2

1. **The gospel keeps us from looking down on others (v. 3).** Paul reminded Titus that he—and all believers—was once just like the people Titus was seeking to welcome into the faith. We all were once lost, hopeless, and living for nothing else than to fulfill our next desire. When we remember that we are no better than those we are seeking to welcome, then we will look on others with compassion rather than judgment.

2. **The gospel reminds us what is possible (vv. 4-5).** Paul reminded Titus that all of us, if we are Christians, have a moment of awakening to the truth of the gospel of Jesus Christ. We are born again, with a new heart, tastes, and desires.

3. **The gospel points us to the future (vv. 6-7).** Thanks to the gospel, we all have a sure hope in the future. We are destined for eternal life with Jesus. We might not be as welcoming as we should be because we have a very temporal view of life. Welcoming others may require us to be uncomfortable or inconvenienced. We might need to step outside our shell. But when eternity is in the balance, these things are shown to be what they truly are: shortsighted objections.

If Titus wanted to create a sustained and empowered work for God on this island, he needed to remember the *why* before he started doing the *what*. The same is true for us. If any ministry we seek to do for God is not grounded in the *why* of the gospel, it will eventually run out of steam. So, if we want to welcome others into the church, we must remember that at one point we ourselves were on the outside looking in. And if God had not rolled out the welcome mat with the life of His own Son, that's where we would have stayed.

Titus 3:8b

8b I want you to insist on these things, so that those who have believed God might be careful to devote themselves to good works. These are good and profitable for everyone.

True, faithful, joy-filled, and sustained ministry to others flows out of the gospel of Jesus. That's because what God has done in us through Jesus always works itself out in good works. This was exactly Paul's point to Titus. Because of the gospel of Jesus, Titus should respond with ministry to others: "These are good and profitable for everyone."

What are some ways you've seen good works really make a difference?

QUESTION #3

Sometimes we have trouble understanding this because we think of the gospel as the way we begin a relationship with God in Christ. This is certainly true, but it's not all the truth.

We often think of the message of the gospel—Jesus lived a perfect life, died a substitutionary death, and rose victoriously from the grave—as the means that enables us to enter the Christian life. That certainly is true, but it doesn't go far enough. The gospel of Jesus Christ doesn't just get us started, we are meant to be driven in daily life by the cross and the resurrection. We don't move past the gospel; we continually dwell and live in the gospel so that it permeates everything we do, including the way we welcome others. At times, we can feel secure and safe in our own friendships and don't want to reach out to others. It may also feel uncomfortable relating to people who look, act, and believe differently than we do. It's in those times we have to remind ourselves of the truth of the gospel. We have to reconnect with the truth that God welcomed us. At some point, we too were strangers and also needed the welcome mat rolled out. By remembering this, we will find new energy to welcome others joyfully into the church.

Titus 3:9-11

⁹ **But avoid foolish debates, genealogies, quarrels, and disputes about the law, because they are unprofitable and worthless. ¹⁰ Reject a divisive person after a first and second warning. ¹¹ For you know that such a person has gone astray and is sinning; he is self-condemned.**

Having spent time in Crete, Paul knew the issues that might distract Titus from his mission. The issues Paul mentioned were of personal preference and self-centeredness, but they were not limited to Crete. We are all tempted to lose our focus and fixate on issues of personal preference.

When we allow personal preference and self-centeredness to creep into ministry, it is destructive to our mission. Still, the temptation is strong to wave the banner of preference in our churches, but by focusing on our self-centeredness, we reveal certain misunderstandings we have about the church:

▶ **Our role in the church.** Churches can engage in all types of arguments that are ultimately trivial. When we argue about carpet colors and worship styles—all matters of personal preference—we show that we really believe the church exists to meet our needs and expectations rather than being the body of Christ for others.

▶ **The composition of the church.** God's desire is to redeem people of every tribe, tongue, and nation to worship Him for all eternity. One of the most convincing things about Christianity during the days of the early church was how the church was made up of different types of people. The fact these individuals were able to worship together despite their personal preferences shows the unifying power of the gospel.

▶ **The nature of the church.** The church is much more than a building for people to worship in. When we gather together, it's as if God places the gathering of His people on display before all the powers in heaven as a showplace of His wisdom. This grand purpose magnifies just how trivial arguments of personal preference are.

> *What steps can we take to redirect debates toward kingdom-focused conversations?*
>
> **QUESTION #4**

> *How can the truths of Titus 3:3-11 help our group be more welcoming?*
>
> **QUESTION #5**

MY PREFERENCES

For each of the following sentences, describe your preferences. Then answer the questions.

I prefer to go to a church service at this time of day:

I prefer to sing/hear this type of music at church:

I prefer to hear more from this person during church:

I think the offering should be taken at this point in the service:

I prefer to sit here when I come to church:

I prefer to sit in/at [chairs/pews/tables]:

Review your list of responses. Could any of your responses become a point of conflict within the church? How does that type of conflict look to people who visit your church?

"Most church members have forgotten what it's like to be a first-time guest!"

—DR. THOM S. RAINER

LIVE IT OUT

Our lives should be a welcome mat into the church. We can assume that posture when we focus on the gospel. Conduct a reality check by choosing one or more of the follow applications.

▶ **Remind yourself.** Identify a practical way you can remind yourself of the gospel this week.

▶ **List.** Create a list of things that, in your opinion, would be the ideal way to "do" church. Identify which of those items are integral to the mission and ministry of the church and which ones are based on your personal preferences.

▶ **Befriend.** Make an intentional effort to befriend someone who is different than you. Consider what you can do to make that person feel welcome in your church.

Our church may not be able to meet every person's expectations, but if we are transformed by the gospel, we can be a welcome mat rather than a stumbling block to others.

My thoughts

2 | OPEN ARMS

When have you felt like "the new kid"?

QUESTION #1

Welcoming others goes beyond a friendly handshake.

THE BIBLE MEETS LIFE

Moving is hard. In addition to packing your belongings and boxing up your memories, you also have to acclimate to new surroundings. A new grocery store. A new traffic pattern. Even a new local news team on TV. Everything is new and nothing is familiar.

That won't last forever. What is new will eventually become familiar. Things will become comfortable as you adjust to your new normal. We all love familiarity because what is familiar is comfortable.

That kind of familiarity and comfort can be good when we are adjusting to a new home, but it's dangerous in the life of a Christian.

We naturally gravitate to the people we know best and who are like us. It's easier to interact with people with whom we share a common interest or background. But a problem arises when those friendships drive us to overlook or ignore others, or worse, to show preferential treatment. Jesus, on the other hand, loves all people the same—and we're called to do likewise. We must learn to embrace everyone with open arms.

WHAT DOES THE BIBLE SAY?

James 2:1-4

¹ My brothers and sisters, do not show favoritism as you hold on to the faith in our glorious Lord Jesus Christ. ² For if someone comes into your meeting wearing a gold ring and dressed in fine clothes, and a poor person dressed in filthy clothes also comes in, ³ if you look with favor on the one wearing the fine clothes and say, "Sit here in a good place," and yet you say to the poor person, "Stand over there," or "Sit here on the floor by my footstool," ⁴ haven't you made distinctions among yourselves and become judges with evil thoughts?

The Book of James was written to Christians who were undergoing persecution. James wrote this letter not only to encourage them to remain strong during those difficult times, but also to remind them that faith and obedience is linked together.

It's in this context that James addressed the issue of partiality. These Christians claimed to believe the gospel and follow Jesus, but apparently they were not treating people equally in their congregations, especially regarding wealth. According to James, this was an evil thing to do. This is true for at least three reasons:

1. **Partiality neglects the image of God in fellow humans.** When we show favoritism to one person or group of people over another, we are—whether we realize it or not—subtly neglecting the truth that all human beings have been created in the image of God. Because all of us have been created in God's image, every one of us is worthy of honor and dignity. When we remove some of that honor and dignity, even if it seems like a small thing, we are doing more than exercising our preference for one group or another. We are denying the image of God in the neglected party.

What are some ways we might be tempted to show favoritism today?

QUESTION #2

2. **Partiality sees others as objects to be used.** Why might we show favoritism? In James' illustration of the rich man and the poor man in the fellowship, the reason is simple: we can get something from the rich man. By showing favoritism, we might receive: some of his money, a greater reputation because we are associated with a person of prominence, or his approval which would increase our self-esteem. Whatever the case, we are hoping to gain something from him, which means we are using that person rather than serving and loving him.

3. **Partiality sets us up as judge.** Favoritism is a big deal because it puts us in the place of God. We are determining someone's worthiness based on some preconceived notion because of the person's clothes, money, reputation, or whatever. But we are not equipped to make this judgment. Indeed, only God can look at the heart. When we show partiality, we are putting ourselves in the place of God. We are judging the worth of another.

James 2:5-7

⁵ Listen, my dear brothers and sisters: Didn't God choose the poor in this world to be rich in faith and heirs of the kingdom that he has promised to those who love him? ⁶ Yet you have dishonored the poor. Don't the rich oppress you and drag you into court? ⁷ Don't they blaspheme the good name that was invoked over you?

How do these verses reveal God's character?

QUESTION #3

We might be tempted to think partiality is not that big a deal, but we only think that when we fail to see the heart behind such actions. James has already helped us see that "evil" is not too strong a word to use when describing favoritism. In addition to the evil of treating other people as objects rather than as fellow image-bearers, partiality is also wrong because it runs contrary to the heart of God.

When you begin to consider God's posture toward humanity, an important word comes to mind: grace. Because of His great love for us, God has assumed a posture of grace toward human beings. When we adopt an attitude of favoritism, we are neglecting God's heart of grace in at least two ways:

1. Favoritism makes assumptions based on external appearance. God's grace is not based on how much money we have, how educated we are, or how polished our appearance is. When we show favoritism based on these external qualities, we are implying that someone is either closer to or further away from God's favor. Such an attitude runs contrary to the very definition of grace.

2. Favoritism focuses on what we receive rather than what we can give. Perhaps in James' day, the thinking was that by showing favoritism to these seemingly important people, the congregation might receive financial benefit. In either case, the focus is on what the church might receive. This, too, runs contrary to what grace is: a gift freely given with nothing expected in return.

If we want to adopt the heart of God, then no place remains for partiality and favoritism. We must recognize that it is only by grace that we have been welcomed into His family—and we are to extend that same grace to others.

James 2:8-10

[8] **Indeed, if you fulfill the royal law prescribed in the Scripture, Love your neighbor as yourself, you are doing well. [9] If, however, you show favoritism, you commit sin and are convicted by the law as transgressors. [10] For whoever keeps the entire law, and yet stumbles at one point, is guilty of breaking it all.**

Perhaps the most obvious reason why partiality and favoritism are wrong is because attitudes like these are inconsistent with love. And love is the language the Christian should speak above anything else.

Love God. Love people. That's it. If we do this, then we are doing everything. James called love "the royal law prescribed in Scripture." But as James also pointed out, the opposite is also true—if we fail at love, then we fail at everything else. To show favoritism is to be guilty of all.

> *What is the connection between our relationship with God and our relationship with others?*
>
> **QUESTION #4**

Many times we don't understand how strong our vertical relationship with God is related to our horizontal relationships with others. We know we're supposed to love each other, but a lot of the time doing so seems to be a sheer act of will. Such an attitude entirely misses the connection between our relationship with God and our relationships with others.

We love others not because we force ourselves to do so, but because we are truly in touch with the measure of God's love for us. Since that's true, the opposite is also true: we fail to love others because we fail to believe or understand the fullness or completeness with which we have been loved by God.

When the temptation to show favoritism rises inside us—when we know our tendency is to always favor one group over another—we would do well to remind ourselves that we are all on level ground at the foot of the cross. "There is no one righteous, not even one" (Rom. 3:10). Not even that person or group we tend to favor, and certainly not us. God Himself does not show favoritism; instead, He is building His kingdom from unlikely places and sources. And that should be our attitude.

> *How can the truths of James 2:1-10 help our group be more welcoming?*
>
> **QUESTION #5**

LOVE ANYWAY

What is a practical step you can take to make sure you are prepared to respond appropriately in the situation you chose?

Convince yourself to love anyway!

"Love the Lord your God with all your heart, with all your soul, with all your strength, and with all your mind" and "your neighbor as yourself."

—LUKE 10:27

LIVE IT OUT

We must break out of the huddles of familiarity we have created for ourselves and reach out to any and all God brings our way. Choose one or more of the following applications.

▶ **Pray.** Pray specifically that God would bring you in contact with someone who looks, talks, or thinks differently than you.

▶ **Change seats.** When you gather this week to worship or in your group, intentionally sit somewhere different. Sit next to someone new and engage him or her in conversation.

▶ **Go someplace new.** Don't just wait for someone different to come your way; be proactive and go out of your way to meet someone new. Go to a different area in your community for some everyday task like buying groceries. While you're there, engage someone new in conversation.

It's always easier to surround ourselves with people who are familiar, but we must remember that God loves everyone the same, so we must learn to embrace them all with open arms.

My thoughts

3 | GRACIOUS HOSPITALITY

What's the most interesting place you've stayed on a trip?

QUESTION #1

Ground your service and love in hospitality.

THE BIBLE MEETS LIFE

The world's largest hotel chain owns exactly zero square feet in hotel room space.

Airbnb® was launched in 2007 when two roommates could not afford to pay their rent in San Francisco. In order to make a little extra money to cover their expenses, they had the idea of putting an air mattress in their living room and charging people to stay there. For many, the idea was laughable. Who would pay to sleep in the home of a perfect stranger?

But a decade or so later, Airbnb has three million lodging listings in 65,000 cities and 191 countries. These are real people opening up their homes to strangers and inviting them in. Clearly, the thought of staying in a real home resonates with a lot of folks in a lot of cultures.

Gracious hospitality is nothing new. Being hospitable is, in fact, a very spiritual characteristic. Hospitality is a command and one Christians must embrace if we want to live in a welcoming posture to those coming into the faith. Our graciousness and hospitality to individuals outside our circle of friends attracts people to the gospel we profess.

WHAT DOES THE BIBLE SAY?

1 Peter 4:7

⁷ The end of all things is near; therefore, be alert and sober-minded for prayer.

Hospitality. This was an important quality that characterized the New Testament church; the biblical writers knew it was of great importance.

Hospitality played a key role in the spread of the gospel in the days when the church was just beginning to flourish. When traveling to a new area, people were at the mercy of those who lived in that city. Therefore, Christians took hospitality seriously, and fellow believers who had been displaced were welcomed into the homes and lives of others. This graciousness helped the gospel to spread and take root in these communities.

Times have changed. Despite the fact that we live much of our lives in a "public" way online, most people value privacy more than they did in the past. Though we might put forth a version of ourselves through social media, we still really like our personal space and private time. The nature of hospitality runs counter to this, since hospitality is sharing what we consider to be "personal" with each other in a sacrificial way.

True enough, some gravitate more naturally toward this kind of sharing with others and are bent toward a more "public" approach to life than others. But if we take the words of Scripture seriously, hospitality is more than a character trait that is easier for some to practice than others; it's a command.

To live lives of hospitality, we must begin with prayer. When we pray, we recognize that we are incapable of doing, providing, or manufacturing something on our own. In prayer, we express our reliance on God as our Provider. In prayer, we acknowledge our selfishness and commitment to our own desires are what keep us from sacrificially serving and loving others in the most practical of ways.

So what should we pray for in order to foster an attitude of hospitality?

> *When has your perspective of others been changed because of prayer?*

QUESTION #2

▶ **Pray that God would help us see ourselves as stewards.** One of the reasons we struggle with hospitality is we see ourselves as owners. We own a house. We own our time. We see these things as ours. But we are not owners; we are merely stewards. Everything we have has been given to us by God to use for the sake of His kingdom. *Everything.*

▶ **Pray that God would help us confront our greed.** Another reason we struggle with hospitality is that we are just plain greedy. We hoard our resources for our own personal use and comfort, and our greed makes us reluctant to share them with anyone else. Hospitality is one of the ways God actually breaks us of this mindset.

▶ **Pray that God would bring us opportunities.** If we really want to be obedient to the command of hospitality, then we should be praying for the opportunity to put action to our faith. We should ask God to open our eyes to the needs around us. When we start praying for opportunities to show hospitality, we'll soon be surprised at how many we'll find.

Peter began verse 7 with the reminder that "the end of all things is near." We pray, act in love, and practice hospitality because time is of the essence. The end is near so let's pray, and let's welcome people into our lives. In so doing, we also welcome them into God's kingdom.

1 Peter 4:8-9

8 Above all, maintain constant love for one another, since love covers a multitude of sins. 9 Be hospitable to one another without complaining.

Love is not a feeling; it's a deeply held commitment for the good of another that is always worked out in tangible, practical ways. That's why hospitality is one of the most concrete signs of love. It's a physical, practical way we serve someone else which also costs us something personal.

> *How can our hospitality demonstrate the gospel for others?*
>
> *QUESTION #3*

POSTURING THROUGH PRAYER

One of the best ways we can ready ourselves for hospitality is through prayer. Ask God to reveal the following:

What gifts and abilities has God given you that you could use to serve others?

Do a quick survey of your community and schedule. What other opportunities for hospitality exist now that you are aware of?

Write a brief prayer to God that expresses your heart for hospitality and that recognizes the urgency that is needed.

My Prayer:

_____

_____

_____

_____

"Hospitality opens the door to uncommon community."

—MAX LUCADO

For the Christian, hospitality is not just an act to be performed; it is a lifestyle to be assumed. To understand why that is so, we first need to understand what hospitality is. While certain acts, like making a casserole or opening your home, are indicative of hospitality, the characteristic itself has a deeper meaning and implication than these actions that demonstrate it. The word for hospitality used in this passage comes from the combination of two words: "love" and "stranger." Literally, then, hospitality is the love of strangers.

In the ultimate act of hospitality, God provided a way to welcome us through the death of Jesus Christ. Therefore, hospitality is a characteristic built into the spiritual DNA of all those who have experienced God's divine hospitality. Hospitality, then, compels us to put aside our own interests, lay down our own desires, and welcome the needs of others ahead of our own. Jesus did that for us, and we're to do likewise.

During His earthly life, Jesus practiced the essence of hospitality, which is sacrificing something of your own to welcome others. Hospitality is not merely a set of actions; it's a posture of living that grows out of "constant love for one another." Let's love like Jesus, assuming a posture of sacrifice to welcome others into our lives.

1 Peter 4:10-11

[10] Just as each one has received a gift, use it to serve others, as good stewards of the varied grace of God. [11] If anyone speaks, let it be as one who speaks God's words; if anyone serves, let it be from the strength God provides, so that God may be glorified through Jesus Christ in everything. To him be the glory and the power forever and ever. Amen.

God gives His children spiritual gifts—not for our own sake, but for the sake of building others up. He gives us gifts to be used in service. When we exercise our gifts for the sake of the body of Christ, we can do so with confidence, knowing God will give us what we need to do so.

The power and provision is God's responsibility; He does all the enabling we will need. But we have a responsibility as well. Rather than being passive bystanders to God's enabling power, we must act in faith to make the most of what God is providing.

Think of this divine/human partnership like a sailboat. The only way a sailboat is going to be propelled through the water is by the force of the wind. But the diligent sailor does not simply wait for the wind to blow. Rather, the sailor positions the sail so it can make the most of the wind when it does start to blow.

So it is with us and the enabling power of God. For our hospitality and other spiritual gifts to make a difference, we need the empowerment of God. But we have the responsibility to position our lives in such a way that we are ready to make the most of what God is going to do in and through us.

When God works through us using our spiritual gifts, many things happen. The most obvious one is that other people benefit. They might benefit from an encouraging word, from an act of service, or from the gracious welcome of hospitality. But that's not all that happens. Our willingness to be used by God to serve other people implicitly communicates important things we believe to be true:

> ▶ **We are speaking about our provision.** Exercising hospitality will cost us in time, energy, resources, and even privacy. When we willingly allow God to use us to demonstrate hospitality, we are testifying that we believe God to be our great Provider.

> ▶ **We are speaking about our contentment.** Hospitality requires us to share with others, which often means we will have to make do with less for ourselves. But when we choose this posture of hospitality, we are testifying about our personal contentment.

> ▶ **We are speaking about our future.** God is not merely redeeming individuals; He is building a people for His own glory. These people will live together with Him for all eternity. Heaven will not be lived in isolation, but in community. When we welcome others in, we are living out a small foretaste of what's to come in the future.

When has someone else's hospitality encouraged you in your walk with Christ?

QUESTION #4

How can the truths of 1 Peter 4:7-11 help our group be more welcoming?

QUESTION #5

LIVE IT OUT

Hospitality might be easier for some than others but we are all commanded to be hospitable. Choose one of the following applications.

▶ **Greet.** Arrive at church a few minutes early this week. Spend extra time in the area outside the worship room to make sure you say hello and meet people you don't know.

▶ **Host a group.** Look for an opportunity to host a small group in your home or to be a greeter in your Bible study group.

▶ **Share a meal.** Dedicate one Sunday each month to be a day when you will invite someone into your home for lunch. Make this a regular rhythm in your life.

Regardless of whether our natural personality is welcoming or not, we are compelled by how God has welcomed us to extend the same welcome to others.

My thoughts

4 | INTENTIONAL LOVE

When has a wrong turn led to a pleasant surprise?

QUESTION #1

Go out of your way to love others.

THE BIBLE MEETS LIFE

What do the following have in common?

▶ Alexander Fleming found mold in a petri dish had killed all the bacteria around itself. We now have penicillin.[1]

▶ Percy Spencer walked in front of a magnetron and the peanut butter candy bar in his pocket melted. This led him to create the microwave oven.[2]

▶ On a hike, Georges de Mestral noticed burrs clinging to his pants. This gave him the idea for Velcro®.[3]

All these discoveries were made by accident; they stumbled onto a discovery that would shape part of history going forward.

These may have been happy accidents, but we can't approach the Christian life that way. Following Jesus does not mean stumbling around in the dark hoping for a good result; following Jesus is an intentional act of obedience. If we desire to be a welcoming people, we won't get there by accident. We will only get there through intentional acts of love. It's a standard of love that goes the extra mile.

WHAT DOES THE BIBLE SAY?

Luke 10:25-28

25 Then an expert in the law stood up to test him, saying, "Teacher, what must I do to inherit eternal life?" 26 "What is written in the law?" he asked him. "How do you read it?" 27 He answered, "Love the Lord your God with all your heart, with all your soul, with all your strength, and with all your mind;" and "your neighbor as yourself." 28 "You've answered correctly," he told him. "Do this and you will live."

Jesus used a powerful story to teach us what it looks like to intentionally love others. But to fully understand the meaning of the story, we must understand the occasion when Jesus told it. The story of the good Samaritan was prompted by a question from an expert in the law.

Some questions are pure in their intent. A person typically desires to know a certain piece of information. That information may even be vital to their health or future. In those cases, just asking the question is an act of humility, for in asking we are admitting our shortcoming in not knowing the answer ourselves.

But that's not the attitude that prompted this question. This expert of the law asked a critically important question, but his question was not born of a humble search. This was instead a prideful examination. He had no desire to hear truth from Jesus; instead, he "stood up to test him." His question was meant to demean and discredit Jesus.

Jesus answered the question by asking one of His own, and knowing the man was an expert in the law, He asked the question in terms of the law. This gave the man what he really wanted: an opportunity to showcase his knowledge. In this man's mind, he already knew the answer to his own question. To inherit eternal life, he must love God with his entire being, and love his neighbor as himself. Indeed, this was the right answer, though the young expert failed to understand the true implications of those commands.

> *When has your love for God prompted you to love other people?*
>
> *QUESTION #2*

One such implication is that these two great loves which summarize all the commands of Scripture are linked together. Our love for God comes first from the fact that He loved us (see 1 John 4:19), and that love drives and shapes our love for others. That means our love for others should have these qualities:

▸ **We love others unreservedly.** God is no respecter of persons. Nationality, ethnicity, education level, and social standing do not limit or regulate His love. We should not withhold our love for someone based on external appearance, familiarity, or any other reason.

▸ **We love others sacrificially.** How much did God's love for us cost Him? It cost Him the life of His One and only Son. This is the highest price He could have paid; yet God was willing to back up His love with action.

▸ **We love others proactively.** God's love is not an ivory tower kind of love. Rather, He got down in the muck and mire of a sinful world in the person of Jesus Christ. He did not wait for humanity to cry out to Him, but instead He took the initiative to come to us. We also must be the first movers.

Luke 10:29-32

29 But wanting to justify himself, he asked Jesus, "And who is my neighbor?" 30 Jesus took up the question and said: "A man was going down from Jerusalem to Jericho and fell into the hands of robbers. They stripped him, beat him up, and fled, leaving him half dead. 31 A priest happened to be going down that road. When he saw him, he passed by on the other side. 32 In the same way, a Levite, when he arrived at the place and saw him, passed by on the other side.

FINDING MARGIN

	Sun.	Mon.	Tues.	Wed.	Thurs.	Fri.	Sat.
Morning							
Noon							
Afternoon							
Evening							
Night							

Mark the places you might use to intentionally display love for others. List some options for ways to best spend that time ministering to others, then prioritize them from 1-3 based on which you are most likely to be able to accomplish this month.

"I give you a new command: Love one another. Just as I have loved you, you are also to love one another!"

—JOHN 13:34

Although Jesus answered the man's question, he was not satisfied. He wanted a further qualification from Jesus. If this man were to love his neighbor, then he wanted to know specifically who that was.

The spirit behind his second question: "Who is my neighbor?" is one of minimalism. The man wanted to know how little he could do with this "love your neighbor" stuff and still be OK. Jesus calls us to love in a much different way. Jesus wants to move us from asking, "What's the least I have to do?" to "What else can I do?"

Jesus doesn't give us a glimpse into the thoughts behind the actions of the priest and the Levite, but we surely can imagine all the ways they might have justified their indifference and apathy.

The point is that both men found excuses *not* to help, and it probably wasn't that difficult to do so. Indifference was the easier way—and it still is. Every day, we encounter people who are spiritually injured and bleeding on the proverbial roadside. We can always find an excuse for passing them by.

> *In what ways do we sometimes justify not helping others in need?*
>
> QUESTION #3

▶ It's none of my business.

▶ I wouldn't know what to say.

▶ I've got enough problems of my own.

▶ Someone else is better equipped.

At the bottom of any excuse we offer is a simple failure to love. This is the dirty truth of indifference—it is not an attitude of neutrality; it is an outright denial of the call to love others as God loves them.

We would do well to recognize our tendency to find excuses. Once we recognize our own internal pull toward indifference, then we will be more prepared to actively fight against such indifference. And we fight indifference through intentional—and many times uncomfortable—acts of tangible love.

Luke 10:33-37

33 But a Samaritan on his journey came up to him, and when he saw the man, he had compassion. 34 He went over to him and bandaged his wounds, pouring on olive oil and wine. Then he put him on his own animal, brought him to an inn, and took care of him. 35 The next day he took out two denarii, gave them to the innkeeper, and said, 'Take care of him. When I come back I'll reimburse you for whatever extra you spend.' 36 "Which of these three do you think proved to be a neighbor to the man who fell into the hands of the robbers?" 37 "The one who showed mercy to him," he said. Then Jesus told him, "Go and do the same."

The lawyer whose questions led to this story had sought to justify himself by doing as little as possible for his neighbors. Jesus gave the Jews a hero they hated because of his race, and yet this Samaritan went above and beyond any reasonable expectation in order to help someone in need. As we look at the intentional acts of love and mercy the Samaritan showed, we are to do the same.

▶ **Be people of awareness.** We must make it our business to be people of awareness. We must educate ourselves on the lives and issues facing the individuals we encounter each day. Until we do so, we will always simply be passing on the other side of the road.

▶ **Be people of compassion.** The Samaritan in the story wasn't motivated because a crowd was watching him. He was internally motivated by compassion. We should be asking God to fill us with the same love and compassion that motivated Jesus to be the friend of the friendless.

▶ **Be people of margin.** The reason the Samaritan was able to give of his resources is because he had built in some margin. This is a good lesson for us because most of us have zero margin in our lives. We should assume God will bring needs into our path every day that will cost us and arrange our schedules, finances, and other resources to have room to meet those needs.

When has someone taken risks or made sacrifices to demonstrate God's love to you?

QUESTION #4

How can the truths of Luke 10:25-37 help our group be more welcoming?

QUESTION #5

LIVE IT OUT

We might accidentally stumble upon a situation that requires our help, but none of us are going to accidentally love and serve someone else. We only do this with intention. Choose one of the following applications.

▶ **Get to know someone.** How intentional are you when you come to worship? This week, intentionally seek out someone you aren't familiar with and ask that person a few questions to get to know him or her.

▶ **Trim your schedule.** How much margin is in your life? Evaluate your finances and schedule, and cut back so that you have room to meet the needs of others God brings your way.

▶ **Encourage someone.** Who is one person you know that is struggling, but to whom you have been indifferent? Schedule a time to sit down with that person this week.

Let's gear our lives so that we are ready to intentionally take advantage of opportunities God brings our way to express His love to others.

My thoughts

1. "Sir Alexander Fleming-Biographical," *Nobelprize.org*, https://www.nobelprize.org/nobel_prizes/medicine/laureates/1945/fleming-bio.html.

2. Steven Tweedie, "How the Microwave Was Invented by a Radar Engineer Who Accidentally Cooked a Candy Bar in His Pocket," *Business Insider*, July 3, 2015, http://www.businessinsider.com/how-the-microwave-oven-was-invented-by-accident-2015-4.

3. Jake Swearingen, "An Idea that Stuck: How George de Mestral Invented the Velcro Fastener," *The Vindicated*, November 1, 2016, http://nymag.com/vindicated/2016/11/an-idea-that-stuck-how-george-de-mestral-invented-velcro.html.

> **What's the best forgery, fake, or fraud you've seen or heard about?**

QUESTION #1

Authentic joy flows from a relationship with Jesus.

THE BIBLE MEETS LIFE

Between 1590 and 1613, William Shakespeare wrote close to forty plays that are still performed around the world. So in 1795, when William-Henry Ireland produced documents supposedly written by Shakespeare, the world took notice. Several experts authenticated the documents. When Ireland "found" a previously unknown Shakespearean play called *Vortigern and Rowena*, it was immediately put into production. But the first performance revealed a play so bad that fighting broke out and Ireland was revealed as a fraud.[1]

Ireland didn't find these documents at all. He had cleverly aged parchment paper and learned to forge the handwriting of the famous playwright; eventually however, these works were seen for the forgeries they were. At some point, inauthenticity will always be revealed—even when it is in a Christian's attitude.

Most of us can be polite and friendly when we have to, but genuine joy calls for something deeper. People can detect the difference between a superficial "I'm glad to see you" and authentic joy. We cannot manufacture such genuine joy, but we will possess it when we're consumed with the gospel and the love of Christ.

WHAT DOES THE BIBLE SAY?

1 Thessalonians 1:1-3

¹ Paul, Silvanus, and Timothy: To the church of the Thessalonians in God the Father and the Lord Jesus Christ. Grace to you and peace. ² We always thank God for all of you, making mention of you constantly in our prayers. ³ We recall, in the presence of our God and Father, your work produced by faith, your labor motivated by love, and your endurance inspired by hope in our Lord Jesus Christ.

The Christian church did not have a peaceful beginning in Thessalonica, the capital and largest city of Macedonia. Paul, Silas, and Timothy visited the city on Paul's second missionary journey. Many people in Thessalonica accepted the missionaries' message of Christ, but the Jewish community incited a mob to attack the house where the missionaries were staying. (See Acts 17:1-5.)

Nonetheless, the church had gotten off to a good start overall, but then Paul had to leave hoping the good work of the gospel would continue. Paul was not disappointed. He later received word that the new Christians in Thessalonica were continuing to grow in the faith and were persevering despite the continued persecution they were experiencing.

So great was Paul's joy that he wrote the letter we know as 1 Thessalonians. In these first few verses, you can hear not only his relief but also the great joy Paul felt after hearing what was going on there.

The Thessalonian Christians were working, laboring, and enduring. Paul was certainly thankful, and his thankfulness carried a sense of confidence that all these things would continue. But how could Paul be confident that these believers, young in their faith—believers he had spent so little time with—would continue working, laboring, and enduring?

> *What do work, labor, and endurance have to do with faith, love, and hope?*
>
> *QUESTION #2*

His confidence was not in the Thessalonians' ability. They were just ordinary people, weak and fallible. No, his confidence was in the foundation of their work, labor, and endurance. Faith produced their work. Love motivated their labor. Hope inspired their endurance.

Because the foundation was sure, the outward actions would continue. It is important for us to remember that any outward signs of our faith—like joy, for example—are ultimately dependent on the firmness of our foundation.

The battle and the work of the Christian are to be done at the heart level. And though it might not be as immediately gratifying as focusing on the beauty at the surface, this deep soul work where the Holy Spirit molds and shapes us is where we find our true strength. Long before our joy is expressed outwardly to others it is formed inwardly through our faith, hope, and love.

1 Thessalonians 1:4-6

⁴ For we know, brothers and sisters loved by God, that he has chosen you, ⁵ because our gospel did not come to you in word only, but also in power, in the Holy Spirit, and with full assurance. You know how we lived among you for your benefit, ⁶ and you yourselves became imitators of us and of the Lord when, in spite of severe persecution, you welcomed the message with joy from the Holy Spirit.

The foundation of our entire being is built on our salvation in Christ. These Christians believed the gospel, received the Holy Spirit, and were confident they had been accepted and welcomed into the family of God. As a result of that sure foundation, they had a joy that was unshakeable.

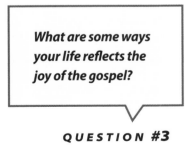

What are some ways your life reflects the joy of the gospel?

QUESTION #3

If we are truly confident in our salvation in Christ, then we should have a true and authentic joy that is apparent to all who come in contact with us—and such joy is infectious to those around us. This authentic joy is one of the greatest ways we can have a welcoming heart and spirit. With such joy we truly desire for others to experience the same certainty and joy that we have experienced.

What does this kind of joy look like? Authentic joy that arises out of salvation in Christ has at least these three characteristics:

1. **Authentic joy does not wax and wane with circumstances.** We tend to associate joy with what's going on during our day. But joy is deeper than a mere sentiment or emotion; joy does not ebb and flow with our circumstances. Joy finds its source in God alone.

2. **Authentic joy is more solid and stable than the rising sun.** Because joy comes from God, our unshakable Rock (see Ps. 18:2), we can know our true source of joy will never be shaken. That means we are never without hope.

3. **Authentic joy is not found in immediate gratification but by pushing past it.** Everywhere we turn, the promise of happiness is held out for us, but joy is much deeper. Author C. S. Lewis wrote: "We are half-hearted creatures, fooling about with drink and sex and ambition when infinite joy is offered us, like an ignorant child who wants to go on making mud pies in a slum because he cannot imagine what is meant by the offer of a holiday at the sea. We are far too easily pleased."[2]

How does demonstrating joy in difficult circumstances make a difference in the kingdom?

QUESTION #4

1 Thessalonians 1:7-10

[7] **As a result, you became an example to all the believers in Macedonia and Achaia.** [8] **For the word of the Lord rang out from you, not only in Macedonia and Achaia, but in every place that your faith in God has gone out. Therefore, we don't need to say anything,** [9] **for they themselves report what kind of reception we had from you: how you turned to God from idols to serve the living and true God** [10] **and to wait for his Son from heaven, whom he raised from the dead—Jesus, who rescues us from the coming wrath.**

The Thessalonian believers presented just such a joyful witness. Paul reported that the believers in this city had become an example for others throughout the region and beyond. These believers had a reputation—a joyous designation that pointed to Christ and served as an invitation for others to embrace what they had. What a wonderful thing!

Perhaps you desire that too, but the circumstances of life seem to constantly threaten living in such joy. Maybe we can begin by reminding ourselves daily of a few things:

▶ **Remember what you deserve.** One of the great enemies of joy is entitlement. Entitlement creeps in when we look around at our circumstances and begin to foster the idea that we deserve something better than the situation or circumstance in which we find ourselves.

▶ **Remember what you have.** Another enemy of joy is comparison. We can get so caught up in our own covetousness that we simply don't have any room for joy. In those moments we should reflect on what we truly have.

▶ **Remember what was paid.** A great price has been paid for our salvation. We were not rescued from our empty way of life by silver or gold; no, it was by something much more valuable. Jesus was given for our sake. And in response, we begin to cultivate hearts that are no longer entitled. Instead, our hearts burn white hot with joy for the glory of the Lamb that was slain.

> *How can the truths of 1 Thessalonians 1:1-10 help our group be more welcoming?*

QUESTION #5

AUTHENTIC JOY

Using the words below, put a box around the actions Paul took toward the Thessalonians and a circle around the actions for which the Thessalonians were known:

Prayed	**Turning from idols**	**Faithful work**
Thanked God	**Serve the one, true God**	**Remembered**
Enduring hope	**Wait for Jesus' return**	**Loving labor**

Now underline the actions that produce authentic joy in your life as you interact with other people for Christ.

How will these affect the way you live out your week?

"Joy is the serious business of Heaven."

— C.S. LEWIS

LIVE IT OUT

A faithful walk nurtures authentic joy with Christ. Choose one of the following applications.

▶ **Thank someone.** Who is one person in your life who lives with authentic joy? Write a note and thank that person for his or her example.

▶ **Grow in joy.** Take a hard look at the three suggestions for growing your joy (see page 44). Write them on index cards and place them in spots where you will see them on a daily basis.

▶ **Journal your thanks.** Because joy is linked with gratitude, begin a "thankful" journal. Each day for the next month write down something you are thankful for and watch your joy begin to grow.

Happiness and a plastic smile can be manufactured easily enough, but time and circumstances will reveal the phoniness behind it. Authentic joy, on the other hand, will shine through, for it is rooted in what God has done for us in Christ.

My thoughts

---

1. Doug Stewart, "To Be…Or Not: The Greatest Shakespeare Forgery," *Smithsonian*, June 2010, https://www.smithsonianmag.com/history/to-beor-not-the-greatest-shakespeare-forgery-136201/.
2. Lewis, C.S., *The Weight of Glory*, (Harper One, 1949), 26.

6 | GOING OUT

Where do you feel most safe?

QUESTION #1

Engaging others with the gospel means going where they are.

THE BIBLE MEETS LIFE

Increasingly, people are devoting anywhere from around forty thousand to more than eight million dollars to install a bunker on their property. The philosophy behind spending this much money is simple: in case of disaster, people want to be safe and comfortable, and to potentially be safe and comfortable for a long period of time.[1]

You may not be ready or able to shell out millions of dollars to install a bunker, but we can all relate to the desire for safety, stability, and comfort. These are all good desires, but if they are incorporated into a church, they can be counterproductive to the church's mission.

Though the majority of churches in America are not closed to outsiders; many have a "bunker" mentality. They stay safe and warm on their own church property. They want other people to visit, however, and even get involved. They may even make guests feel welcome—*if* they come to church.

Unfortunately, most people never come to the church building. We need to come out of our church bunker, go where people are, and extend the invitation.

WHAT DOES THE BIBLE SAY?

Acts 16:6-8

6 They went through the region of Phrygia and Galatia; they had been forbidden by the Holy Spirit to speak the word in Asia. 7 When they came to Mysia, they tried to go into Bithynia, but the Spirit of Jesus did not allow them. 8 Passing by Mysia they went down to Troas.

Paul never had a bunker mentality. His entire life was devoted to going out and meeting people wherever they were with the message of the gospel. Sometimes that meant meeting Jews in the synagogue; other times it meant meeting Gentiles in the marketplace. How Paul presented the message of the gospel differed from occasion to occasion because he adapted his method to fit the audience (see 1 Cor. 9:20-22), but his core philosophy remained the same: don't wait for them to come to you; go to where they are.

It's important for us to see just how eager Paul was to reach others. He wanted to go into Asia, but the Spirit stopped him from doing so. This is the opposite of what many of us experience. We are hesitant to share because we're concerned with getting the words right. So we look for some kind of divine confirmation that *this* is the right moment, and *this* is the right person. We should have the opposite perspective. The gospel should be so readily on the tip of our tongues that we reckon any moment is the right moment and any person is the right person. This was how Paul approached his life and ministry.

What might keep us from having that same kind of passion and perseverance in sharing the gospel?

▶ **Prosperity.** One of the most subtle but dangerous enemies of our passion and perseverance in evangelism is prosperity. Prosperity inevitably makes us feel comfortable—and the more comfortable we are, the more hesitant we are to do anything that might disrupt that sense of comfort. The temptation is to simply keep the status quo.

> *When have you been thankful God told you "no"?*

QUESTION #2

▶ **Busyness.** Going out to reach others for Christ will take time—a lot of time. And time is a scarce resource in our culture. If we want to be about the business of evangelism, then the time to witness to others is going to have to come from somewhere. We may have to rethink all our activities and rearrange our priorities to make time to do so.

▶ **Faithlessness.** One final obstacle to our passion and perseverance in evangelism is simply a lack of faith. Do we *really* believe the gospel has the power to change people's lives? Perhaps our own lack of faith is one of the reasons it is sometimes difficult for us to tell others about Christ.

Compounding these obstacles of prosperity, busyness, and our lack of faith is the simple reality that sharing the gospel is not always a one-time conversation. Rather, it often requires an investment of time in a relationship that provides several opportunities not only to talk about the good news about Jesus, but also to faithfully model the gospel.

Acts 16:9-10

⁹ During the night Paul had a vision in which a Macedonian man was standing and pleading with him, "Cross over to Macedonia and help us!" ¹⁰ After he had seen the vision, we immediately made efforts to set out for Macedonia, concluding that God had called us to preach the gospel to them.

Who in our community might be saying, "Cross over... and help us!" today?

QUESTION #3

ENGAGING OTHERS

From the list of words below, circle all the words that describe how you feel when you think about sharing the gospel with someone else.

unqualified	petrified	comfortable	experienced	inexperienced
unsure	blessed	cared	afraid	nervous
grateful	terrified	ready	personal	empowered
unashamed	failure	rejection	desire	embarrassment
weakness	inadequate	guilt	joy	prepared

Write a prayer asking God for wisdom and courage to engage others with the gospel wherever they are.

"To the weak I became weak, in order to win the weak. I have become all things to all people, so that I may by every possible means save some."

—1 CORINTHIANS 9:22

Paul was constantly looking for an opportunity to share the gospel, and the Holy Spirit was faithful to give him a dream that specifically directed him to cross over into Macedonia. Paul immediately obeyed.

You probably won't have a dream directing you to travel to a particular place, but the truth is you don't need one. Jesus has already given us the clear command to go into the entire world and share the gospel as His witnesses. (See Matt. 28:19; Acts 1:8.) What we need more than a dream is a posture of ready awareness.

To assume this posture of ready awareness, we must keep certain truths before us:

▶ **Jesus is coming back.** It could be today. Like now. Or now. Or now. Or maybe tomorrow. That's kind of the point. Jesus taught a series of parables that all centered on His return and how His people should prepare. (See Matt. 24:4-41.) Then He declared in Matthew 24:42: "Therefore be alert, since you don't know what day your Lord is coming."

▶ **Opportunities are all around us.** God has gone before us to prepare opportunities for us to speak and demonstrate the truth of the gospel. "For we are His workmanship, created in Christ Jesus for good works, which God prepared ahead of time for us to do" (Eph. 2:10).

▶ **We have the tendency to drift.** No one drifts toward Jesus. Instead, like a boat not anchored in the middle of the sea, unless we are actively and alertly fighting against it, we will always move away from our original position. "For this reason, we must pay attention all the more to what we have heard, so that we will not drift away" (Heb. 2:1).

Acts 16:11-15

¹¹ From Troas we put out to sea and sailed straight for Samothrace, the next day to Neapolis, ¹² and from there to Philippi, a Roman colony and a leading city of the district of Macedonia. We stayed in that city for several days. ¹³ On the Sabbath day we went outside the city gate by the river, where we expected to find a place of prayer. We sat down and spoke to the women gathered there. ¹⁴ A God-fearing woman named Lydia, a dealer in purple cloth from the city of Thyatira, was listening. The Lord opened her heart to respond to what Paul was saying. ¹⁵ After she and her household were baptized, she urged us, "If you consider me a believer in the Lord, come and stay at my house." And she persuaded us.

From this simple story, we learn a few key things about sharing Christ with others:

▶ **Sharing Christ requires a verbal testimony.** An old saying states: "Preach the gospel at all times. If necessary, use words." Speaking the truth of the gospel has little effect if the words are not backed up by a lifestyle that exemplifies the love and compassion of Jesus. But this statement is erroneous if implying words aren't necessary. Preaching the gospel always requires words.

▶ **Responding to Christ requires the work of God.** Paul and his companions did their part—they gave a faithful witness to the truth of the gospel. Lydia and the other women at the river were listening intently. And that's when "the Lord opened her heart to respond to what Paul was saying." This is an important truth: responding to Christ requires the work of God.

▶ **Sharing Christ produces ripples.** After Lydia believed, the effects of that gospel encounter began to ripple outward. Lydia believed—and so did her whole household! It was through those ripples that the believing community in Philippi grew and Philippians was eventually written. We should not underestimate the power a single conversation can have in the hands of God.

How would you describe God's part and our part in leading others to Christ?

QUESTION #4

How can the truths of Acts 16:6-15 help our group be more welcoming?

QUESTION #5

LIVE IT OUT

The church should *not* be a bunker. Instead, we must go where others are. Choose one of the following applications:

▶ **Pray about fear.** What is your biggest fear or apprehension about sharing the gospel with someone else? Share that fear with someone in your group and ask him or her to pray for you to overcome it.

▶ **Seek the opportunity.** Who is one person in your relational circle you know does not believe the gospel? Pray and look for the opportunity to share with that person.

▶ **Serve together.** Brainstorm with your group about practical ways you can go out together to serve and speak the word of the gospel.

To truly be a welcoming church, and to obey the commission of Jesus, we cannot sit around and wait for people to come into the church building. We must instead take the initiative and go to where the people are.

My thoughts

1. Madeline Stone, "The Upcoming Election Is Causing Luxury Bunker Sales to Soar," *Business Insider*, October 8, 2016, http://www.businessinsider.com/luxury-bunker-sales-are-soaring-due-to-election-2016-10.

HOSPITALITY AS A SPIRITUAL GIFT

BY DARRYL WOOD

A journey to a strange place creates uneasiness in many people. A friendly smile, warm welcome, and relaxed surroundings ease the stress of travel. People have practiced such hospitality in various ways throughout history. The first century of the Christian church was no exception.

Background of the Term

The term often used for "hospitable" and "hospitality" developed from a compound of the Greek words *xenos* (stranger, foreigner) and *philos* (friend). The resulting word, *philoxenia* (hospitality) or *philoxenos* (hospitable), came to refer to "treating a stranger as a friend" demonstrated through concern for those outside a person's usual relationship circle.

Hospitality appears to have been interwoven into the Hellenistic culture. The ancients practiced hospitality long before the Christian church began. Early Greek city-states extended care to representatives of other friendly cities. They recognized a humanitarian obligation to provide aid to others. A religious motive drove the concept in some cases.[1] Aristotle, Homer, and other ancient Greek writers mentioned hospitality and hospitable people.[2] The early church developed in an environment that knew hospitable treatment of strangers.

The Jewish roots of the early Christians also influenced them toward hospitality. The concept of hospitality appeared often in the Old Testament.[3] Frequently care extended not only to strangers but also to their animals. Provision of hospitality came with an unspoken expectation of reciprocity. In spite of this, though, Judaism tended to see strangers as a potential threat to Hebrew life and faith.

First-Century Practices

Due to increased travel opportunities, the need for showing hospitality expanded in the first century. Travel boomed for three interdependent reasons. First, massive road building efforts facilitated greater mobility of the population. Second, trade and commercial development in the Roman Empire necessitated travel. Third, the growing Roman presence supported a peaceful environment that made travelers more secure. Certainly crime still existed. The Romans, however, worked to protect routes for travel and trade.

Having a hospitable nature ... should flow naturally from a Christ-like outlook.

Movement from place to place increased the demand for food and shelter along travel routes. The lodging industry failed to advance adequately. Few inns of any size or quality existed. The mobile population sometimes received help from kind people on their route. Thus the tendency toward hospitality that pervaded the Greek culture expanded with the times.

Welcoming travelers as an expression of hospitality was one of many actions the early church took in practicing charity toward those in need. Other charitable expressions included care for church leaders, widows, orphans, the sick, prisoners, slaves, and support for other churches, as well as further acts of kindness.[4]

Association of hospitality with the journey motif remains significant, though, for two reasons. First, the term's origin relates to care of strangers or aliens. That concept seems to be the purest application of the term. Second, hospitality supported expansion of the early church. The practice enabled Christians to convey the gospel message beyond their local communities.[5]

The New Testament includes numerous references that imply the practice of hospitality. Jesus modeled and taught self-sacrificial love as the primary basis for Christian living. Love engendered virtues such as generosity, compassion, respect for people, and hospitality. Jesus set the tone for the exercise of Christian hospitality to strangers, although He did not use the word specifically. He also received hospitality throughout His ministry.[6]

As they traveled from place to place, early Christian missionaries relied on fellow believers' hospitality. The New Testament contains several calls to hospitality and examples of it for missionary travelers and others.[7]

Additionally the early church probably met mostly in homes due to the lack of public meeting places. Hospitable believers opened their residences to the brethren. The practice facilitated teaching from guest instructors.[8] Some writers commended hospitality to the churches as a part of their Christian ministry.[9]

Gift or Duty?

The key to understanding hospitality revolves around how the church interpreted the concept. Was it a spiritual gift the Holy Spirit gave to some believers? Or was being hospitable every Christian's duty?

All believers receive a gift or gifts from the Holy Spirit as a result of His grace. A simple definition of a spiritual gift is a divine, special ability the Holy Spirit gives to a Christian to be used for the common good of the church. The most inclusive New Testament gift lists come from Paul's writings.[10] Other New Testament passages identify gifts on a more limited basis. Ultimately God determines the types of gifts and their recipients.

The New Testament never names hospitality specifically as a spiritual gift. Believers practicing hospitality in the early church, however, supports the notion that it was one of the gifts. Both Paul and Peter mentioned it in connection with other spiritual gifts. (See Rom. 12:6-13; 1 Pet. 4:8-11.)

Practicing the gift of hospitality meant using this divinely ordained ability to share unselfishly and joyfully with others, including strangers, in support of relationship building and spiritual growth in the church community. Writing to persecuted Christians, Peter explained the necessity for "intense love" within the church fellowship. Simon Peter pointed to the importance of service gifts to undergird Jesus' love command. (See 1 Pet. 4:10.) Possibly he intended "be hospitable" in verse 9 to be an example of one of those service gifts. Practicing hospitality supported ministry both to Christian exiles suffering from persecution and missionaries attempting to expand the gospel beyond their home areas.

If "hospitality" is one of the spiritual gifts, does that prohibit its practice by believers not gifted with that divine, special ability? No. The New Testament shows that some practices are the duty of all believers. For example, each Christian should live out the works of kindness, evangelism, giving, faith, and hospitality—even if these are not the believer's spiritual gift. Although other believers will not be as proficient in practicing hospitality as one gifted in it, every Christian should be hospitable.

Is hospitality a gift or duty? It is both. The New Testament indicates that some are gifted in hospitality. They possess a heightened aptitude to build relationships, welcome guests, and provide for their support—and to do so joyfully. Those gifted with hospitality enhance church ministry. Every believer will not be the consummate host like those gifted with hospitality. Having a hospitable nature, though, should flow naturally from a Christ-like outlook.

1. Gustav Stahlin, "xe/noç, xeni/a, xeni/zw, xenodce/w, filoxeni/a, filo/xenoß" (xenos, foreign) in *Theological Dictionary of the New Testament* [TDNT], ed. Gerhard Friedrich, trans. and ed. Geoffrey W. Bromiley, vol. 5 (Grand Rapids: Eerdmans, 1967), 17-18.

2. Aristotle, On Virtues and Vices 5.5, 8.3 in *The Loeb Classical Library*, trans. H. Rackham, (Cambridge, MA: Harvard Univ. Press, 1935), 495, 503; *The Odyssey of Homer* 6.121, 8.576, trans. S. H. Butcher and A. Lang (New York: MacMillan, 1927), 96, 133. See Stahlin, "xe/noß" (xenos, foreign) in TDNT 5:17-18 for other references to hospitality and Greek writings.

3. For examples see Genesis 18:1-8; 19:1-11; 24:14-22; Judges 19:10-25.

4. Adolf Harnack, *The Expansion of Christianity in the First Three Centuries*, trans. and ed. James Moffatt, vol. 1 (New York: Books for Libraries, 1904), 190-249.

5. Donald Wayne Riddle, "Early Christian Hospitality: A Factor in Gospel Transmission," *Journal of Biblical Literature* 57, no. 2 (June 1938), 143-46.

6. See Matthew 25:35. For examples of Jesus' reception of hospitality, see Matthew 9:10; Mark 7:24; 14:3; Luke 7:36; 10:38.

7. See Acts 16:15; 18:27; Romans 12:13; 1 Timothy 3:2; 5:10; Titus 1:8; Hebrews 13:1-2; 1 Peter 4:8-9; 3 John 5-6.

8. The Didache 10.3; 11.1; 12.1-2.

9. Clement of Rome, "The First Epistle of Clement to the Corinthians 1.2,"; "The Shepherd of Hermas."

10. See Romans 12:6-8; 1 Corinthians 12:8-10,28; Ephesians 4:11.

Darryl Wood is pastor of First Baptist Church, Vincent, Alabama.

GENERAL INSTRUCTIONS

In order to make the most of this study and to ensure a richer group experience, it's recommended that all group participants read through the teaching and discussion content in full before each group meeting. As a leader, it is also a good idea for you to be familiar with this content and prepared to summarize it for your group members as you move through the material each week.

Each session of the Bible study is made up of three sections:

1. THE BIBLE MEETS LIFE.

An introduction to the theme of the session and its connection to everyday life, along with a brief overview of the primary Scripture text. This section also includes an icebreaker question or activity.

2. WHAT DOES THE BIBLE SAY?

This comprises the bulk of each session and includes the primary Scripture text along with explanations for key words and ideas within that text. This section also includes most of the content designed to produce and maintain discussion within the group.

3. LIVE IT OUT.

The final section focuses on application, using bulleted summary statements to answer the question, *So what?* As the leader, be prepared to challenge the group to apply what they learned during the discussion by transforming it into action throughout the week.

The *Welcome Home* leader guide contains several features and tools designed to help you lead participants through the material provided.

QUESTION 1—ICEBREAKER

These opening questions and/or activities are designed to help participants transition into the study and begin engaging the primary themes to be discussed. Be sure everyone has a chance to speak, but maintain a low-pressure environment.

DISCUSSION QUESTIONS

Each "What Does the Bible Say?" section features six questions designed to spark discussion and interaction within your group. These questions encourage critical thinking, so be sure to allow a period of silence for participants to process the question and form an answer.

The *Welcome Home* leader guide also contains follow-up questions and optional activities that may be helpful to your group, if time permits.

DVD CONTENT

Each video for *Welcome Home* features Michael Kelly and Dr. Thom Rainer discussing the primary themes found in the session. We recommend you show this video in one of three places: 1) At the beginning of the group time, 2) After the icebreaker, or 3) After a quick review and/or summary of "What Does the Bible Say?" A video summary is included as well. You may choose to use this summary as background preparation to help you guide the group.

The leader guide contains additional questions to help unpack the video and transition into the discussion. For a digital leader guide with commentary, see the "Leader Tools" folder on the DVD-ROM in your leader kit.

For helps on how to use *Bible Studies for Life,* tips on how to better lead groups, or additional ideas for leading, visit: ***ministrygrid.com/web/BibleStudiesforLife.***

SESSION 1: REALITY CHECK

The Point: Our lives should serve as a welcome mat into the church.

The Passage: Titus 3:3-11

The Setting: After the apostle Paul was released from his first imprisonment in Rome (AD 60-62), he continued his missionary work, taking his Gentile co-worker, Titus, along with him. One of the areas they evangelized was the island of Crete. When the apostle moved on, he left Titus behind to appoint elders in every town. (See Titus 1:5.) Paul wrote his letter to Titus around AD 63 to remind Titus of the qualifications necessary for the elders, to describe the aspects of new life in Christ, and to encourage Titus to teach sound doctrine and to rebuke those in the church who were spreading false doctrine.

QUESTION 1: What makes a house feel like a home?

> *Optional activity:* In advance of your group meeting, locate a welcome mat and put it at the door where members will enter. Stand at the door and welcome group members with a handshake as they arrive. Direct them to a table where you have arranged drinks and snacks.

Video Summary: Almost all churches start out well; they are focused on leading people to Christ, serving them, and helping them grow in Christ. Unfortunately, if we are not careful, the church can gradually drift from being Christ-centered to becoming inwardly-focused. Are you walking in the shoes of others? If you are welcoming a nonbeliever, you may have an opportunity in the future to let him or her see Christ in your life. If you are welcoming a believer, you may have the opportunity to be that instrument that works in his or her life to a greater extent. Our actions are centered on the opportunity to share the gospel.

▶ WATCH THE DVD SEGMENT FOR SESSION 1. THEN USE THE FOLLOWING QUESTIONS AND DISCUSSION POINTS TO TRANSITION INTO THE STUDY.

- How would you describe your experiences of being new in a church?
- In what ways are you walking in the shoes of those who are now where you once were? How are you using your own experiences to help others feel welcome?

WHAT DOES THE BIBLE SAY?

▶ ASK FOR A VOLUNTEER TO READ ALOUD TITUS 3:3-11.

Response: What's your initial reaction to these verses?

- What do you like about the text?
- What questions do you have about these verses?

▶ TURN THE GROUP'S ATTENTION TO TITUS 3:3-8A.

QUESTION 2: How have you personally experienced the kindness and love of God?

By answering this question, group members will not only have an opportunity to share personal stories but also acknowledge and reflect on the powerful impact of the kindness and love of God.

> *Optional follow-up:* What are the different elements of the gospel present in these verses?

▶ MOVE TO TITUS 3:8B.

QUESTION 3: What are some ways you've seen good works really make a difference?

Sharing and storytelling represent great ways for growing as a group. This question creates an environment for sharing relative to the message of this week's lesson and biblical text.

> *Optional follow-up:* What's the difference in being saved by good works and devoting oneself to good works?

▶ CONTINUE WITH TITUS 3:9-11.

QUESTION 4: What steps can we take to redirect debates toward kingdom-focused conversations?

This application question is included so that the group can share action steps. It serves as a reminder of the importance of being prepared and promotes the need to act on biblical principles.

> *Optional follow-up:* How can we reject a divisive person while still reflecting God's grace?

QUESTION 5: How can the truths of Titus 3:3-11 help our group be more welcoming?

Use this question as an opportunity for group members to identify practical steps for positive actions based on opportunities that are already available to your group. Try to steer them away from talking theory; encourage them to get practical.

> *Optional activity:* Direct group members to complete the activity, "My Preferences," on page 13 to help them understand how our preferences can impact the church.

Note: The following question does not appear in the Bible study book. Use it in your group discussion as time allows.

QUESTION 6: How has God used the good works in someone else's life to influence you?

Answering this question gives group members an opportunity to share a personal story about how the fruit of another impacted their own life for Christ.

LIVE IT OUT

Our lives should be a welcome mat into the church. We can assume that posture when we focus on the gospel. Encourage group members to conduct a reality check this week by choosing one or more of the follow applications:

- **Remind yourself.** Identify a practical way you can remind yourself of the gospel this week.

- **List.** Create a list of things that, in your opinion, would be the ideal way to "do" church. Identify which of those items are integral to the mission and ministry of the church and which ones are based on your personal preferences.

- **Befriend.** Make an intentional effort to befriend someone who is different than you. Consider what you can do to make that person feel welcome in your church.

Challenge: We might think our churches are welcoming, but the reality can be entirely different. Many people have heard Jesus is a friend of sinners and God loves the world. They have been led to believe the people in church are friendly. Yet when they enter the building, they find something entirely inconsistent with those things they have heard. As you prepare for church on Sunday, ask God to show you what you can do to make your church a more welcoming place for others.

Pray: Ask for prayer requests and ask group members to pray for the different requests as intercessors. As the leader, conclude by thanking the Lord for the gift of His church. Ask God for His eyes and His encouragement that we would be a more welcoming place for others.

SESSION 2: OPEN ARMS

The Point: Welcoming others goes beyond a friendly handshake.

The Passage: James 2:1-10

The Setting: The Letter of James was written by James, the brother of the Lord Jesus, probably some time between AD 50 and AD 60. Very little is known about the audience to which James wrote, but his teachings are clear. In chapter 2 of his letter, James addressed the issue of showing favoritism to the rich over the poor when they visited this group of believers.

QUESTION 1: When have you felt like "the new kid"?

Emphasize the way comfort and personal preferences hinder our connection with others by reading or summarizing the text as well as The Point.

> *Optional activity:* During the study of James 2:1-4, only call on, acknowledge, and talk to people who have a similar trait that you select, such as having brown eyes or black hair, wearing tennis shoes or jeans, or those wearing (or not wearing) a watch. Make it very obvious that you are showing partiality toward certain people, even to the point of totally ignoring others. To make this really effective, use a trait that those who would normally talk, ask questions, and/or respond don't have. Inform your group that the way you interact with them is going to be a bit "different" today. When you get to James 2:5-7, identify the preferences you displayed and discuss how showing partiality can make people feel unwelcome.

Video Summary: It's only natural that we gravitate to individuals we know best and with whom we have the most in common. There's nothing wrong with interacting with those who share a common interest or background. The problem arises when those friendships drive us to treat others differently or exclude them all together. Welcoming others with open arms requires us to give up our rights, our comfort, and what we want for the sake of the body. If we are really a functioning part of the body of Christ, we will always be thinking about the needs of others.

▶ WATCH THE DVD SEGMENT FOR SESSION 2. THEN USE THE FOLLOWING QUESTIONS AND DISCUSSION POINTS TO TRANSITION INTO THE STUDY.

- In what ways have you seen mission drift at your church?
- What specific steps can you take this week to help you see others through the Lord's eyes?

WHAT DOES THE BIBLE SAY?

▶ ASK FOR A VOLUNTEER TO READ JAMES 2:1-10.

Response: What's your initial reaction to these verses?

- What questions do you have about these verses?
- What do you hope to learn this week about seeing people as Jesus sees them?

▶ TURN THE GROUP'S ATTENTION TO JAMES 2:1-4.

QUESTION 2: What are some ways we might be tempted to show favoritism today?

We are all faced with the temptation of showing favoritism at one time or another. Identifying how we have successfully and unsuccessfully dealt with this issue is the first step in gaining confidence that we're equipped to move forward and love others as we are loved.

   Optional follow-up: What motivates people to show partiality and favoritism?

▶ MOVE TO JAMES 2:5-7.

QUESTION 3: How do these verses reveal God's character?

This question requires that group members interpret this Scripture passage for themselves as a way to move them toward life application.

   Optional follow-up: What does it look like on a practical level to be rich in faith?

▶ CONTINUE WITH JAMES 2:8-10.

QUESTION 4: What is the connection between our relationship with God and our relationship with others?

This question gives group members an opportunity to consider how their relationship with God can and will impact their relationships with others. Take this opportunity to point out that what they believe to be true about God not only affects them personally but also affects their relationship with God and others.

   Optional follow-up: In what ways—positive or negative—do you think your understanding of how God loves you has impacted your ability to love others?

QUESTION 5: How can the truths of James 2:1-10 help our group be more welcoming?

Use this question as an opportunity for group members to identify practical steps for positive actions based on opportunities that are already available to your group. Try to steer them away from talking theory; encourage them to get practical.

   Optional activity: Direct group members to complete the activity, "Love Anyway," on page 21 to help them relate to the difficulty we have expressing love sometimes.

Note: The following question does not appear in the Bible study book. Use it in your group discussion as time allows.

QUESTION 6: Why is love so important to the life of a church?

By answering this question, group members should be able to connect the need of an individual to feel love with the responsibility of the church to show others the same love God has shown us.

LIVE IT OUT

We must break out of the huddles of familiarity we have created for ourselves and reach out to any and all God brings our way. Challenge group members to choose one or more of the following actions to take this week.

- **Pray**. Pray specifically that God would bring you in contact with someone who looks, talks, or thinks differently than you.

- **Change seats.** When you gather this week to worship or in your group, intentionally sit somewhere different. Sit next to someone new and engage him or her in conversation.

- **Go someplace new.** Don't just wait for someone different to come your way; be proactive and go out of your way to meet someone new. Go to a different area in your community for some everyday task like buying groceries. While you're there, engage someone new in conversation.

Challenge: It's always easier to surround ourselves with people who are familiar, but we must remember that God loves everyone the same, so we must learn to embrace them all with open arms. As you prepare for church this week, be willing to step out of your comfort zone. Ask God to help you be sensitive to what others truly need. Be willing and place yourself in a position to greet others with more than just a handshake.

Pray: Ask for prayer requests and ask group members to pray for the different requests as intercessors. As the leader, conclude by thanking the Lord for loving us even when we are unlovable. Ask Him to help us see the best in others and to love them well—even when we have difficulty doing that.

SESSION 3: GRACIOUS HOSPITALITY

The Point: Ground your service and love in hospitality.

The Passage: 1 Peter 4:7-11

The Setting: Peter was one of Jesus' twelve apostles. (See Mark 3:16.) He became a leader in the early church and eventually was martyred under the Roman emperor Nero about AD 64. Probably a few years earlier, Peter wrote the letter we call 1 Peter to a group of churches in Asia Minor (modern Turkey). Peter encouraged them to stand strong and to realize the hope they had in Jesus Christ, even as they faced persecution and suffering.

QUESTION 1: What's the most interesting place you've stayed on a trip?

> *Optional activity:* Direct group members to "The Bible Meets Life" on page 24. Before moving on with the rest of the study, spend a few minutes reading or summarizing the text and emphasizing that hospitality is a command we are to obey.

Video Summary: We tend to evaluate ourselves based on what we believe, but we evaluate others based on what they do. Those outside the church do the same thing. We can have the right doctrines, but it's how we live out those truths that make a difference to those around us. Jesus said, "By this everyone will know that you are my disciples, if you love one another" (John 13:35). Our graciousness and hospitality to those outside our circle of friends attracts people to the gospel we profess.

▶ WATCH THE DVD SEGMENT FOR SESSION 3. THEN USE THE FOLLOWING QUESTIONS AND DISCUSSION POINTS TO TRANSITION INTO THE STUDY.

- How would you define hospitality in your own words?
- What is it about your life that attracts others to the Lord?

WHAT DOES THE BIBLE SAY?

▶ ASK FOR A VOLUNTEER TO READ ALOUD 1 PETER 4:7-11.

Response: What's your initial reaction to these verses?

- What questions do you have about these verses?
- What new application do you hope to get from this passage?

▶ TURN THE GROUP'S ATTENTION TO 1 PETER 4:7.

QUESTION 2: When has your perspective of others been changed because of prayer?

This question invites members of the group to share a personal story. Answers will vary based on experience. Be prepared to lead the discussion by sharing an experience of your own.

> *Optional follow-up:* What's the connection between the end of all things and being hospitable?

▶ MOVE TO 1 PETER 4:8-9.

QUESTION 3: How can our hospitality demonstrate the gospel for others?

This question asks group members to interpret the biblical text in terms of how showing hospitality can demonstrate the gospel to others. Encourage them to look beyond the words.

> *Optional activity:* Direct group members to complete the activity, "Posturing Through Prayer," on page 27 to help them ready themselves for hospitality through prayer.

▶ CONTINUE WITH 1 PETER 4:10-11.

QUESTION 4: When has someone else's hospitality encouraged you in your walk with Christ?

Sharing their personal experiences with each other can help group members see and feel the impact hospitality can have in our lives. Encourage them to go one step further and identify specific actions that influenced their walk with Christ.

> *Optional follow-up:* How has God equipped our group to love and serve others?

QUESTION 5: How can the truths of 1 Peter 4:7-11 help our group be more welcoming?

Use this question as an opportunity for group members to identify practical steps for positive actions based on opportunities that are already available to your group. Try to steer them away from talking theory; encourage them to get practical.

Note: The following question does not appear in the Bible study book. Use it in your group discussion as time allows.

QUESTION 6: What obstacles can prevent us from demonstrating hospitality?

Answering this question requires group members to examine the things in their own lives that have kept them from seeking opportunities to demonstrate hospitality to others. Remind them that they aren't alone as you encourage their honesty.

> *Optional activity:* Write the word HOSPITALITY on the board. Provide several sticky notes and a pen to each group member. Instruct members to think for a couple of minutes about applications for biblical hospitality in the context of your small group. Explain that the purpose of this activity is to generate as many ideas as possible. Encourage group members to write down ideas, one per sticky note, and then attach his or her notes to the board. After everyone has participated, review the ideas. Lead the group to select two or three ideas to begin to put into place. Call for volunteers to take ownership of each idea and be responsible for leading the group to get it done.

LIVE IT OUT

Hospitality might be easier for some than others but we are all commanded to be hospitable. Encourage group members to carry out one of the following applications this next week:

- **Greet**. Arrive at church a few minutes early this week. Spend extra time in the area outside the worship room to make sure you say hello and meet people you don't know.

- **Host a group.** Look for an opportunity to host a small group in your home or to be a greeter in your Bible study group.

- **Share a meal.** Dedicate one Sunday each month to be a day when you will invite someone into your home for lunch. Make this a regular rhythm in your life.

Challenge: Being hospitable is a very spiritual characteristic. Hospitality is a command and one Christians must embrace if we want to live in a welcoming posture to those coming into the faith. Look for opportunities this week to show graciousness and hospitality to individuals outside your circle of friends.

Pray: Ask for prayer requests and ask group members to pray for the different requests as intercessors. As the leader, conclude by thanking the Lord for the way He has welcomed us into His family. Ask Him for the wisdom and insight to welcome others in the same way.

SESSION 4: INTENTIONAL LOVE

The Point: Go out of your way to love others.

The Passage: Luke 10:25-37

The Setting: The time of Jesus' earthly ministry was drawing to a close. Therefore, Jesus determined that it was time for Him to journey to Jerusalem, where He would suffer, die, and rise from the dead. (See Luke 9:51; see also vv. 21-22,44.) During this journey, an expert in the law (a scribe) approached Jesus, asking Him what he (the scribe) must do to inherit eternal life.

QUESTION 1: When has a wrong turn led to a pleasant surprise?

> *Optional activity:* Direct class participants to pair up, ideally with someone they don't know extremely well. Explain that the partners will have four to five minutes to have intentional conversations to discover some new things about one another. Encourage them to talk about where they were born, where they grew up, the craziest thing they have ever done, any interesting hobbies or pets, their favorite foods, and/or other things some people may not know about them. After five minutes, call time. Ask for volunteers to share one thing they learned about their partner that they didn't already know. **Ask:** What is one thing you could take away from this activity to help you get to know others?

Video Summary: Anyone can be nice, and the world applauds random acts of kindness. Random acts of kindness are a good thing, but they are not enough. It's easy to be nice and kind when we feel like it, but the needs of others are not always convenient. When we go out of our way to help someone or build a relationship, we are living by the higher standard Jesus calls us to: a standard of love that goes the extra mile. A standard of love like that of the good Samaritan.

▶ WATCH THE DVD SEGMENT FOR SESSION 4. THEN USE THE FOLLOWING QUESTIONS AND DISCUSSION POINTS TO TRANSITION INTO THE STUDY.

- In the video message, Dr. Rainer says, "Intentionality is God's Spirit leading us to do and say what we would not do in our own power." How have you seen this play out in your own life?
- How have you seen this play out through your small group?

WHAT DOES THE BIBLE SAY?

▶ ASK FOR A VOLUNTEER TO READ ALOUD LUKE 10:25-37.

Response: What's your initial reaction to these verses?

- What do you like about the text?
- What new application do you hope to receive about going the extra mile to love others?

▶ TURN THE GROUP'S ATTENTION TO LUKE 10:25-28.

QUESTION 2: When has your love for God prompted you to love other people?

This question invites members of the group to share specific instances when God's love has prompted them to love others. If members seem to feel awkward sharing stories of their own actions, be prepared to lead with one of your own.

> **Optional follow-up:** How does Jesus' answer seem to differ from what the expert in the law had in mind?

▶ MOVE TO LUKE 10:29-32.

QUESTION 3: In what ways do we sometimes justify not helping others in need?

Answering this question requires group members to examine their own lives for times they have justified not helping others and the reasons why. Encourage them to be honest and to listen for what they can learn from other group members as well.

> **Optional follow-up:** How does our church answer the question, "Who is my neighbor?"

▶ CONTINUE WITH LUKE 10:33-37.

QUESTION 4: When has someone taken risks or made sacrifices to demonstrate God's love to you?

This question provides another opportunity for group members to share from personal experience. It will also help them make the connection between the impact of someone demonstrating God's love for them and the importance of them doing the same for others.

> **Optional follow-up:** What obstacles stood in the way of the Samaritan demonstrating love for his neighbor?

QUESTION 5: How can the truths of Luke 10:25-37 help our group be more welcoming?

Use this question for group members to identify practical steps for positive actions based on opportunities already available to your group. Try to steer them away from talking theory; encourage them to get practical.

> **Optional activity:** Direct group members to complete the activity, "Finding Margin," on page 35 to help them plan for opportunities to display love for others.

Note: The following question does not appear in the Bible study book. Use it in your group discussion as time allows.

QUESTION 6: What does it mean to you to love others proactively?

This question allows group members the opportunity to define and then share in their own words what it looks like to be proactive with their love for others. Encourage them to be specific in their responses.

LIVE IT OUT

We might accidentally stumble upon a situation that requires our help, but none of us are going to accidentally love and serve someone else. We only do this with intention. Challenge group members to choose one of the following applications to help them be intentional about helping others this week:

- **Get to know someone.** How intentional are you when you come to worship? This week, intentionally seek out someone you aren't familiar with and ask this person a few questions to get to know him or her.

- **Trim your schedule**. How much margin is in your life? Evaluate your finances and schedule, and cut back so that you have room to meet the needs of others God brings your way.

- **Encourage someone.** Who is one person you know that is struggling, but to whom you have been indifferent? Schedule a time to sit down with that person this week.

Challenge: Following Jesus does not mean stumbling around in the dark hoping for a good result; following Jesus is an intentional act of obedience. If we desire to be welcoming people, we won't get there by accident. We will only get there through intentional acts of love. It's a standard of love that goes the extra mile. Position yourself this week so that you are ready to intentionally take advantage of opportunities God brings your way to express His love to others.

Pray: Ask for prayer requests and ask group members to pray for the different requests as intercessors. As the leader, conclude by thanking God for having gone out of His way to love us the way He has. Ask Him for boldness and passion to love others with that same intention— the kind that can only come from His Holy Spirit at work in us.

SESSION 5: AUTHENTIC JOY

The Point: Authentic joy flows from a relationship with Jesus.

The Passage: 1 Thessalonians 1:1-10

The Setting: Paul wrote his first letter to the believers at Thessalonica in approximately AD 50, about 18 years after Jesus' death and resurrection. This makes 1 Thessalonians both one of the earliest of Paul's letters and one of the earliest writings in the New Testament. As such, it provides one of the earliest glimpses of the first-century Christian community, with its emphasis on faith and love.

QUESTION 1: What's the best forgery, fake, or fraud you've seen or heard about?

> *Optional activity:* In advance of your group meeting, prepare to show the video for Rend Collective's "Joy" to help the group focus on this week's topic. If you have someone in your group who enjoys leading worship, invite him or her to lead the group in singing along. Then lead the group in an opening prayer. (Note: A link to the video may be found at BibleStudiesforLife.com/AdultExtra.)

Video Summary: Most of us can muster a smile and be polite—even friendly—when we have to. But a genuine joy in the other person's presence calls for something deeper in us. The other person can tell the difference between a superficial greeting and true, authentic joy. We can only possess this genuine joy when we're consumed with Christ. Happiness depends on happenings or circumstances. Joy is a peace and contentment in the Lord that defies circumstances.

▶ WATCH THE DVD SEGMENT FOR SESSION 5. THEN USE THE FOLLOWING QUESTIONS AND DISCUSSION POINTS TO TRANSITION INTO THE STUDY.

- When have you mistaken happiness for joy? How did you discover the difference?
- In what ways has true joy freed you to serve others?

WHAT DOES THE BIBLE SAY?

▶ ASK FOR A VOLUNTEER TO READ 1 THESSALONIANS 1:1-10.

Response: What's your initial reaction to these verses?

- What questions do you have about these verses?
- What new application do you hope to get from this passage?

▶ TURN THE GROUP'S ATTENTION TO 1 THESSALONIANS 1:1-3.

QUESTION 2: What do work, labor, and endurance have to do with faith, love, and hope?

This question requires members to interpret the biblical text and then look beyond the words of the passage to discover what can be learned about God's promises to us and our responsibility to others.

> *Optional follow-up:* When have your relationships with others inspired your faith in God?

▶ MOVE TO 1 THESSALONIANS 1:4-6.

QUESTION 3: What are some ways your life reflects the joy of the gospel?

This question is designed to help group members apply the truth of the biblical text to their everyday lives and to make adjustments or put in place a more intentional plan if necessary.

> *Optional follow-up:* When have you seen the power of the gospel displayed in someone's life?

QUESTION 4: How does demonstrating joy in difficult circumstances make a difference in the kingdom?

Ask group members to work together to answer this question. By encouraging them to be practical and specific with their responses, they will feel better prepared to demonstrate joy despite their circumstances.

> *Optional follow-up:* How has someone demonstrating joy in the midst of a difficult circumstance impacted your life?

▶ CONTINUE WITH 1 THESSALONIANS 1:7-10.

QUESTION 5: How can the truths of 1 Thessalonians 1:1-10 help our group be more welcoming?

Use this question as an opportunity for group members to identify practical steps for positive actions based on opportunities that are already available to your group. Try to steer them away from talking theory; encourage them to get practical.

> *Optional activity:* Direct group members to complete the activity, "Authentic Joy," on page 45 to help them understand how genuine joy is produced in our lives.

Note: The following question does not appear in the Bible study book. Use it in your group discussion as time allows.

QUESTION 6: What obstacles get in the way of our living with a sense of love and joy?

Answering this question will help group members see the things in their own lives as well as the lives of others they know that have served as obstacles to living out true joy.

LIVE IT OUT

A faithful walk nurtures authentic joy with Christ. Challenge group members to choose one of the following applications for this week:

- **Thank someone.** Who is one person in your life who lives with authentic joy? Write a note and thank that person for his or her example.

- **Grow in joy.** Take a hard look at the three suggestions for growing your joy (see page 44). Write them on index cards and place them in spots where you will see them on a daily basis.

- **Journal your thanks.** Because joy is linked with gratitude, begin a "thankful" journal. Each day for the next month write down something you are thankful for and watch your joy begin to grow.

Challenge: Happiness and a plastic smile can be manufactured easily enough, but time and circumstances will reveal the phoniness behind it. Most of us can be polite and friendly when we have to, but genuine joy calls for something deeper. Ask God to provide you with opportunities this week to share your authentic joy with someone who really needs it. Be ready to explain how your joy is rooted in what God has done for you in Christ.

Pray: Ask for prayer requests and ask group members to pray for the different requests as intercessors. As the leader, conclude by thanking God for the genuine joy we can experience and express because of what He has done for us through Christ. Ask Him for opportunities to express that joy to others in tangible ways this week.

SESSION 6: GOING OUT

The Point: Engaging others with the gospel means going where they are.

The Passage: Acts 16:6-15

The Setting: Acts 15:36–18:22 records the events of Paul's second missionary journey. Acts 16 details how God stopped Paul from going into various regions of Asia Minor. God also gave Paul a vision of a Macedonian man pleading for Paul's help. Recognizing this vision as divine direction, Paul and his companions crossed over to Macedonia and began spreading the gospel message in the region.

QUESTION 1: Where do you feel most safe?

> *Optional activity:* In advance of your group meeting, invite someone from the group to share his or her testimony of coming to Christ. Ask the group member to emphasize the role different people had in bringing him or her to the place of repentance and faith whether through sowing, watering, or reaping at the end.

Video Summary: The majority of churches in America are not closed to outsiders; they want other people to visit and even get involved. But extending a welcome to those who come to us is not enough, because most people never come to the church building. Instead, the church is to go where people are and extend the invitation. Having a heart to welcome means going out, meeting people where they are with the gospel. As the Spirit leads you, God is giving you greater energy to care for others.

▶ WATCH THE DVD SEGMENT FOR SESSION 6. THEN USE THE FOLLOWING QUESTIONS AND DISCUSSION POINTS TO TRANSITION INTO THE STUDY.

- In this week's video, Dr. Rainer listed some practical suggestions to help you meet people where they are:
  1. Be accountable.
  2. Pray, asking God to lead you to people with whom you can share the love of Christ.
  3. Talk about it.
  Spend some time today putting together an action plan for your group using these steps.

WHAT DOES THE BIBLE SAY?

▶ ASK FOR A VOLUNTEER TO READ ALOUD ACTS 16:6-15.

Response: What's your initial reaction to these verses?

- What questions do you have about going out to meet people where they are?

- What new application do you hope to get from this passage?

▶ TURN THE GROUP'S ATTENTION TO ACTS 16:6-8.

QUESTION 2: When have you been thankful God told you "no"?

This question provides group members with an opportunity to share a personal story based on their own life experience and guides them to a better understanding of why God sometimes tells us "no."

> *Optional follow-up:* How does it make you feel when God says "no."

▶ MOVE TO ACTS 16:9-10.

QUESTION 3: Who in our community might be saying, "Cross over… and help us!" today?

Encourage group members to answer this question both as individuals and as a community. What steps can you take to make sure you don't miss those in need?

> *Optional activity:* Direct group members to complete the activity, "Engaging Others," on page 51 to help them consider their responsibility to share Christ with others.

▶ CONTINUE WITH ACTS 16:11-15.

QUESTION 4: How would you describe God's part and our part in leading others to Christ?

This question calls for group members to apply the biblical text as well as identify their part in the process of leading others to Christ. Because this question is broad in scope, be prepared to start the discussion with some ideas of your own.

> *Optional follow-up:* What are some creative ways you've seen others share the gospel?

QUESTION 5: How can the truths of Acts 16:6-15 help our group be more welcoming?

Use this question as an opportunity for group members to identify practical steps for positive actions based on opportunities that are already available to your group. Try to steer them away from talking theory; encourage them to get practical.

Note: The following question does not appear in the Bible study book. Use it in your group discussion as time allows.

QUESTION 6: When have you felt strongly that God was leading you to deliver His message of hope?

This question allows another opportunity for group members to share a personal story. As time allows, encourage them to share details: How did it feel? What did you do about it? What was the outcome?

> *Optional follow-up:* How might God use your group to bring someone else to Christ?

LIVE IT OUT

The church should not be a bunker. Instead, we must go where others are. Encourage group members to choose one of the following applications they will apply this week:

- **Pray about fear.** What is your biggest fear or apprehension about sharing the gospel with someone else? Share that fear with someone in your group and ask him or her to pray for you to overcome it.

- **Seek the opportunity.** Who is one person in your relational circle you know does not believe the gospel? Pray and look for the opportunity to share with that person.

- **Serve together.** Brainstorm with your group about practical ways you can go out together to serve and speak the word of the gospel.

Challenge: To truly be a welcoming church, and to obey the commission of Jesus, we can't sit around and wait for people to come into the church building. We must instead take the initiative and go where people are. Ask God to take you outside the church and show you opportunities to meet others where they are this week. Then watch and wait for God to provide.

Pray: As the leader, close this final session of *Welcome Home* in prayer. Thank God for the privilege of studying His Word throughout this resource. Conclude by thanking God for the ways He worked to lead us to Christ. Ask Him for opportunities in the coming days to speak the gospel boldly so that we might welcome others into His kingdom.

Note: If you haven't discussed it yet, decide as a group whether or not you plan to continue to meet together and, if so, what Bible study options you would like to pursue. Visit LifeWay.com/smallgroups for help, or if you would like more studies like this one, visit BibleStudiesForLife.com/smallgroups.